Puntoons

by Jack Medoff

RUNNING PRESS
Philadelphia, Pennsylvania

Canadian representatives: General Publishing Co., Ltd.,
30 Lesmill Road, Don Mills, Ontario M3B 2T6.

International representatives: Worldwide Media Services, Inc.,
30 Montgomery Street, Jersey City, New Jersey 07302.

9 8 7 6 5 4 3 2 1
Digit on the right indicates the number of this printing.

Library of Congress Cataloging-in-Publication Number 92-53810

ISBN 1-56138-179-9

Edited by David Borgenicht
Cover design by Toby Schmidt
Interior design by Christian Benton
Cover and interior illustrations by Jack Medoff

This book may be ordered by mail from the publisher.
Please add $2.50 for postage and handling.
But try your bookstore first!
Running Press Book Publishers
125 South Twenty-second Street
Philadelphia, Pennsylvania 19103

Preface

I've always had an odd way of looking at things—it may have started with my mother telling me not to play with my food.

As you can see, I like to let my brain meander, and my hand goes along for the ride. It's especially tough when I'm driving because I often wind up thinking—and drawing, and driving—which can be rather dangerous. You'll know what I mean if you ever see the headline,

PUNTOONIST HAS HEAD-ON COLLISION WITH OAK TREE

I've probably drawn hundreds, if not thousands, of these visual puns. I really don't recall what got me started doing them, but here they are. I hope they make you chuckle.

Or at the very least, wince.

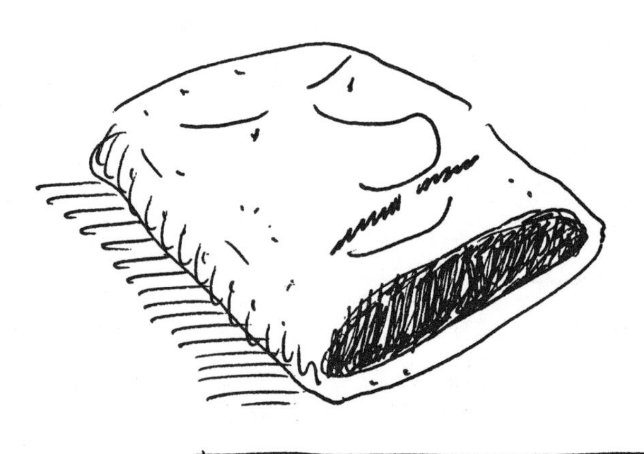

WAYNE NEWTON

MIKE'S
TOE
TRUCK

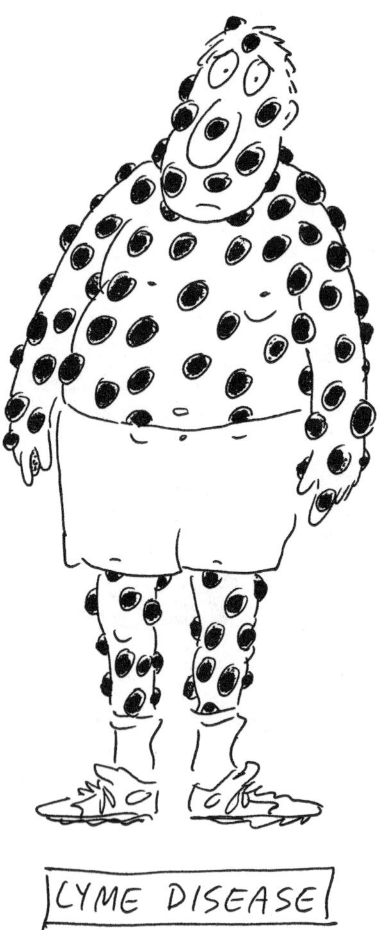
LYME DISEASE

GATOR AID

1 WALNUT

OXYMORON

STRIP CLUB

THE OTTOMAN EMPIRE

DEATH WARMED OVER

RUSSIAN DRESSING

1 COLON
1 SEMI-COLON

CATCHER IN THE RYE

WRITER'S BLOCK

CATCHER IN THE RYE

WRITER'S BLOCK

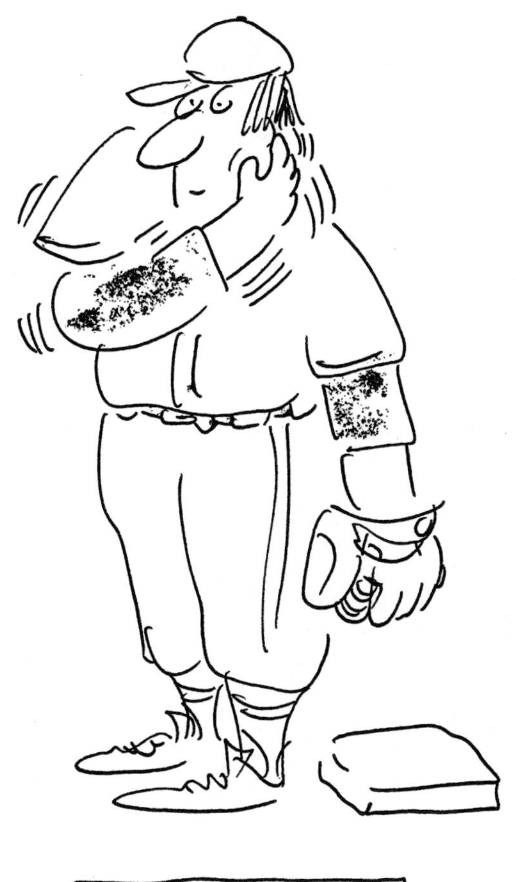

JOCK ITCH

COP ON THE BEAT

HEAD BAND

A SHRINK

HEAD BAND

A SHRINK

KEEP OUT
PRIVATE EYE

FOOT NOTE

ON THE TIP OF ONE'S TONGUE

JUMPING DOWN SOMEONE'S THROAT

WEARING YOUR HEART ON YOUR SLEEVE

JUMPING JACKS

PASSING THE BUCK

EATING CROW

TAKING A GANDER

KISSING ASS

MEAT LOAF

COW LICK

BIG BUCKS

DEER TICK

VICIOUS CIRCLE

STREET SMARTS

MOBILE HOME

DRINKS ON THE HOUSE

DOWN IN THE DUMPS

DEATH TAKES A HOLIDAY

ROCK CLIMBING

A MAN ENJOYING A SPOT OF TEA

PASSING WIND

AD NAUSEAM

BABY-SITTER

TOILET TRAINING

DOG WITH LOOSE STOOL

CATFISH

KITTY LITTER

BEAVER FILMS

DOG-EAT-DOG

THE END OF THE LINE

CUSTER'S
LAST STAND
HOT DOGS -
HAMBURGERS -
FALAFEL -
PIZZA -
SODA -

UNDERGROUND ARTIST

Beethoven's
FIFTH

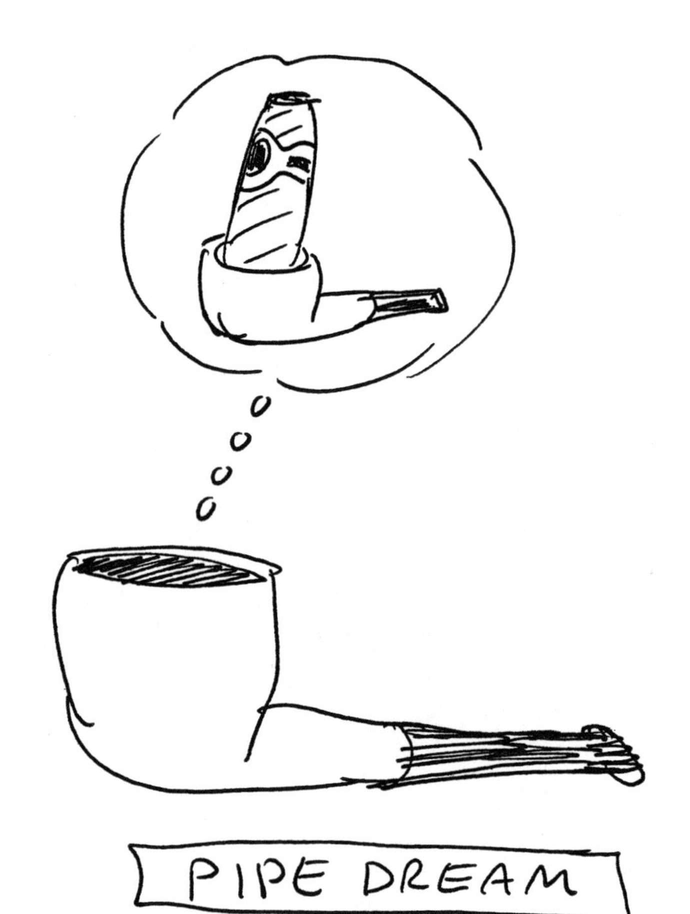

PIPE DREAM

YULETIDE

STOCK CAR

SOAP OPERA

FRENCH TOAST

NAVEL ORANGE

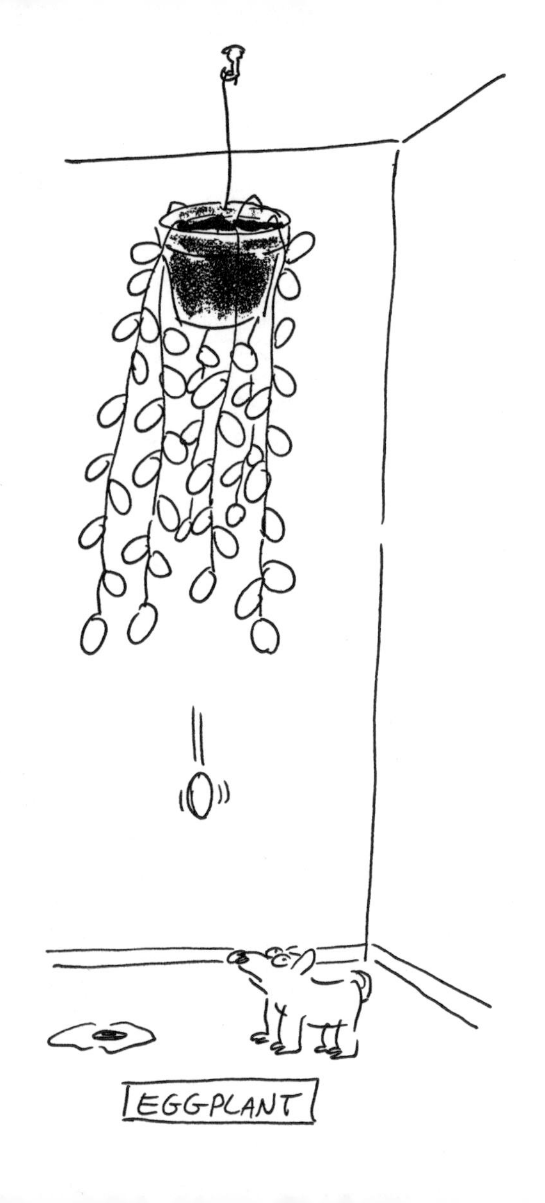
EGGPLANT

LOAN SHARK

ROCK & ROLL

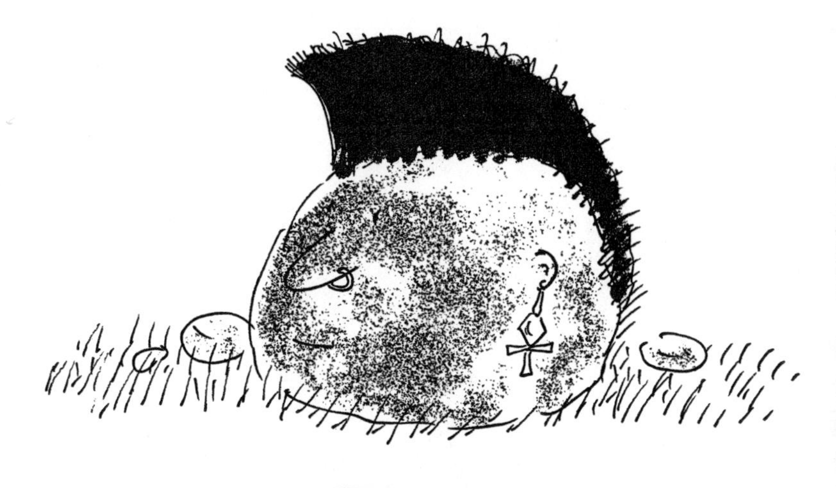

PUNK ROCK

EYE GLASS

EYE SOCKET

A PAIR OF HOOTERS

BRAIN WAVE

GEORGE
WASHINGTON
BRIDGE

FIRE SALE

SKY DIVING

RUNNING ON EMPTY

SELF-STORAGE

BENEATH CONTEMPT

A SLIP OF THE TONGUE

FACELIFT

A COAT OF ARMS

WHAT A SET OF KNOCKERS!

RULE OF THUMB

CHICKEN LITTLE

KILLER WHALE

ANCHORMAN

HUNG JURY

GUT FEELING

BONDHOLDER

FINGER SANDWICHES

SPERM WHALE

SAFE SEX

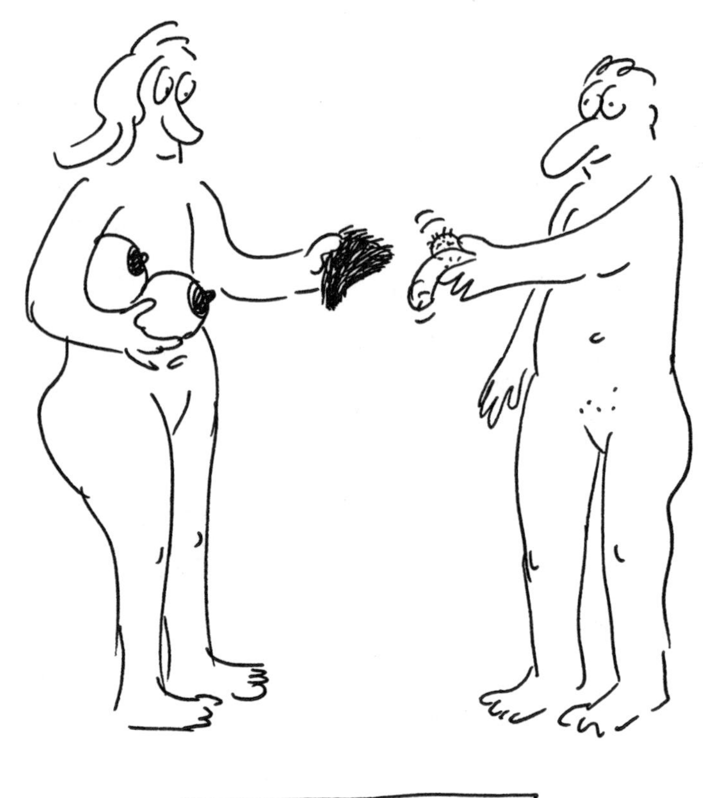

SEX CHANGE

A FREUDIAN SLIP

I MISTLETOE

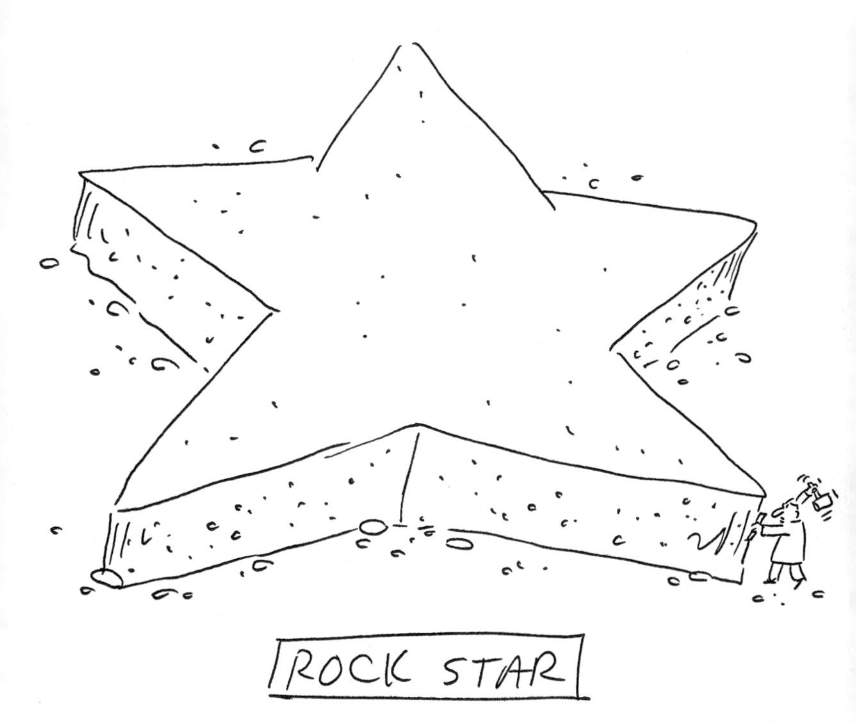

ROCK STAR

PAYING THROUGH THE NOSE

KNEECAP

THE END OF THE ROAD